Learn AJAX

Practical Guide

A. De Quattro

Copyright © 2024

Guide to Ajax

1. Introduction to AJAX

Ajax, short for Asynchronous JavaScript and XML, is a web technology that allows the creation of interactive and dynamic applications without the user having to reload the page every time they want to get new data or interact with the site. This significant improvement in user experience has revolutionized the way people navigate the web and has made it possible to create highly responsive and fast web applications.

The introduction of Ajax was a breakthrough in the world of web development, as it allowed the creation of websites that look more like desktop applications, thanks to its ability to asynchronously update only certain parts of the page without the need to reload the entire web page. This led to a significant improvement in performance and usability of websites, making user interaction more fluid and intuitive.

Ajax is based on a combination of technologies including HTML, CSS, JavaScript, and XML. HTML and CSS are used for the structure and style of the web page, while JavaScript is the programming language that allows managing user interactions and sending asynchronous requests to the server. XML is used for data transmission between the server and the client, although it has largely been replaced by lighter and faster formats like JSON.

The underlying idea of Ajax is to create asynchronous communication between the client and the server, allowing the client to send requests to the server and process responses without having to reload the entire page. This allows updating only the parts of the page that need to be changed, reducing the loading time and improving the user experience.

One of the most common uses of Ajax is the creation of interactive web pages that allow the user to perform operations without having to reload the page. For example, an e-commerce site could use Ajax to update the shopping cart in real time without displaying a new page, or a social network could use Ajax to allow users to comment and share content without updating the entire page.

Furthermore, Ajax is widely used for the creation of complex web applications like Google Maps, Gmail, and Facebook, which leverage the power of this technology to offer an advanced and highly interactive user experience.

2. Knowledge required to use AJAX

AJAX, which stands for Asynchronous JavaScript and XML, is a web technology that allows for sending and receiving data in the background from a server without having to reload the entire webpage. It is widely used in modern web applications to provide a smooth and interactive user experience.

To use AJAX effectively, it is necessary to have familiarity with various web technologies and concepts. Here are some fundamental knowledge requirements for using AJAX:

1. HTML and CSS: HTML is the markup language used to create the structure of a webpage, while CSS is used to define the style and presentation of the page. To use AJAX, it is important to have a solid understanding of HTML and CSS in order to dynamically manipulate the page content.

2. JavaScript: AJAX primarily relies on JavaScript to handle requests and responses from the server asynchronously. Understanding JavaScript is essential for writing client-side code that interacts with the server and updates the page dynamically.

3. XML and JSON: AJAX can be used to exchange data with the server in different formats, including XML and JSON. Knowledge of how to manipulate and interpret data in these formats is essential for using AJAX effectively.

4. HTTP and AJAX: AJAX relies on the HTTP protocol to send requests and receive responses from the server. It is important to understand the different HTTP methods (such as GET, POST, PUT, and DELETE) and HTTP status codes to properly handle AJAX requests.

5. APIs and Web Services: Often, AJAX requests are used to communicate with APIs and web services to retrieve or send data to the server. It is important to be familiar with API documentation and understand how to access and use the provided data.

6. DOM Manipulation: With AJAX, it is possible to dynamically update the page content without reloading the entire page. Being able to manipulate the DOM (Document Object Model) using JavaScript to update page contents effectively is important.

7. Error Handling: With AJAX requests, properly handling errors that may occur during the process of sending and receiving data from the server is crucial. Being able to handle error messages and provide useful feedback to the user in case of issues is important.

To use AJAX effectively, a solid

understanding of HTML, CSS, JavaScript, XML, JSON, HTTP, APIs, DOM manipulation, and error handling is required. With these basic knowledge, it is possible to fully leverage the potential of AJAX to create interactive and dynamic web experiences for users.

3. Simple Interactions in AJAX

AJAX is a web technology that allows web pages to communicate with the server without having to reload the entire page. This is possible thanks to the ability to exchange data in the background between the browser and the server, without interrupting or affecting the user's experience on the page.

Simple interactions in AJAX are very useful for creating dynamic and interactive web pages, where content is updated asynchronously without having to refresh the entire page. Common interactions in AJAX include loading data from a remote server, sending data to a server, and updating specific parts of a page.

An example of a simple interaction in AJAX could be a contact form on a web page. When a user fills out the form and clicks the submit button, the form data is sent to the server without having to reload the entire page. The server processes the data and sends a response, which the browser uses to update only the section of the page related to the contact form, without affecting the rest of the page.

To implement simple interactions in AJAX, you need to use JavaScript to handle asynchronous HTTP requests and manipulate the data received from the server. Below we see an example of how you can create a simple AJAX interaction to dynamically load content from a remote server.

Let's say we have a web page with a button that, when clicked, should load and display data from a remote JSON file. To achieve this functionality, we can use the following JavaScript code:

```javascript
```

```javascript
document.getElementById('load-data-btn').addEventListener('click', function() {
  var xhr = new XMLHttpRequest();
  xhr.open('GET', 'https://api.example.com/data.json', true);
  xhr.onreadystatechange = function() {
    if (xhr.readyState === 4 && xhr.status === 200) {
      var data = JSON.parse(xhr.responseText);
      document.getElementById('data-container').innerHTML = 'Name: ' + data.name + ', Surname: ' + data.surname;
    }
  };
  xhr.send();
});
```

In this code, we are listening for the click

event on the button with the id "load-data-btn". When the user clicks the button, a new instance of the XMLHttpRequest object is created, allowing us to make asynchronous HTTP requests. With the `open` method, we are specifying the type of request and the URL of the JSON file to load.

The `onreadystatechange` method is used to handle the change in the request's state. When the request's state becomes 4 (completed) and the status is 200 (OK), we can access the data received through the `responseText` method, which in this case is a JSON object. We then use the `JSON.parse` method to convert the JSON data into a JavaScript object that we can manipulate.

Finally, we update the content of the section with the id "data-container" with the data obtained from the JSON file, which in this case is the name and surname. This way, when the user clicks the button, the data is loaded in the background and displayed without having to refresh the page.

Simple interactions in AJAX can be implemented in various ways and are very useful for creating user-friendly and dynamic web pages. They can be used to dynamically update content, send and receive data from the server asynchronously, and enhance the user experience on the page. Knowing and using AJAX is therefore essential for developing modern and interactive web applications.

4. Advanced interactions in AJAX

Introduction

Advanced interactions in AJAX represent an effective way to enhance the user experience on a website, allowing to load and display data dynamically without having to reload the entire page. By using technologies like JavaScript and XMLHttpRequest, it is possible to send asynchronous requests to the server and update only the necessary portions of the page, reducing loading times and improving the fluidity of navigation.

In this article, we will explore some of the advanced interactions that can be achieved using AJAX, analyzing practical examples and providing guidelines for implementing these functionalities effectively.

Loading dynamic content

One of the most common uses of AJAX is

loading dynamic content within a web page. This approach allows to update certain sections of the page without reloading the entire page, improving the user experience and reducing loading times.

For example, consider an e-commerce website that displays a list of products. Using AJAX, it is possible to allow the user to filter the list of products based on certain criteria without reloading the page. When the user selects a specific filter, an asynchronous request is sent to the server to retrieve the corresponding products and update the section of the page that displays the results.

To implement this functionality, JavaScript can be used to handle user interaction and send XMLHttpRequest requests to the server. The server will then process the request, return the necessary data, and update the page section using JavaScript.

Updating content based on user interactions

Another advanced feature that can be achieved with AJAX is updating the content of the page based on user interactions, such as hovering over certain elements or selecting an option from a drop-down menu.

For example, consider a website that displays a list of newspaper articles. Using AJAX, it is possible to allow the user to view a preview of the article when hovering over the title, without opening a new page or reloading the entire page.

To implement this functionality, JavaScript events can be used to detect user interactions, such as hovering over an element, and send AJAX requests to retrieve the necessary data and update the page section with the article preview.

Asynchronous loading of files and images

Another advanced feature that can be achieved with AJAX is the asynchronous loading of files and images. This approach allows to improve the loading speeds of the page, allowing the user to view the main content of the page while the files and images are downloaded in the background.

For example, consider a portfolio website that displays a gallery of images. Using AJAX, it is possible to allow the user to navigate through the images without having to wait for all the images in the gallery to fully load. When the user selects an image, an asynchronous request is sent to the server to download only the selected image, allowing the user to view it immediately.

To implement this functionality, JavaScript can be used to handle user interaction and send XMLHttpRequest requests to the server to download the necessary files and images. Once loaded, the page section can be dynamically updated with the downloaded content.

Real-time form validation

Another advanced feature that can be achieved with AJAX is real-time form validation. This approach allows to check and validate the data entered by the user in the page forms in real-time, providing instant feedback and reducing input errors.

For example, consider a contact form on a website. Using AJAX, it is possible to check the form fields as the user fills them out, verifying the correctness of the entered data and providing immediate feedback in case of errors. For instance, if the user enters an invalid email address, an error message can be displayed without submitting the form to the server.

To implement this functionality, JavaScript can be used to detect user input events in the form fields and send asynchronous requests to the server to check the correctness of the entered data. The server will then return a response indicating whether the data is correct or not, allowing to dynamically update the page with the appropriate feedback.

Real-time content updating

Another advanced feature that can be achieved with AJAX is real-time content updating on a webpage, allowing users to view the latest available data without having to manually reload the page. This approach is particularly useful in real-time web applications, such as online chats and news feeds.

For example, let's consider an online chat on a website. Using AJAX, it is possible to update the chat in real-time, showing messages sent by other users without having to reload the page. When a user sends a message, an asynchronous request is sent to the server to store the message and update the chat for all users in real-time.

To implement this functionality, JavaScript can be used to send and receive messages through XMLHttpRequest requests to the server, synchronizing the page content with real-time updated data. The server will then handle storing messages and notify all users of the new chat using AJAX.

Advanced user interaction management

Finally, advanced interactions in AJAX allow for sophisticated features to effectively manage user interactions, improving the usability and interactivity of the website. In this regard, JavaScript libraries like jQuery can be used to simplify AJAX request management and improve page performance.

For example, let's consider an event planning website. Using AJAX and jQuery, users can add, delete, and modify events directly on the page without having to reload the entire page. When a user interacts with an event, asynchronous requests are sent to the server to update the data and display the changes in real-time.

To implement this functionality, jQuery can be used to manage user behaviors and send AJAX requests to the server to save and update event data. The server will then process the requests and return a response indicating whether the operation was successful, allowing for dynamically updating the page with the updated data.

Advanced interactions in AJAX offer numerous possibilities to enhance user experience on a website, allowing for dynamic and interactive data loading and display. By using technologies like JavaScript, XMLHttpRequest, and jQuery, sophisticated features such as dynamic content loading, real-time updating, form validation, and advanced user interaction management can be implemented.

Advanced interactions in AJAX enable the

creation of dynamic and interactive web applications, where data can be sent and received from the server without having to reload the page. This allows for the creation of richer and more responsive user interfaces, where user actions can trigger real-time page updates without interruptions or unnecessary reloads.

An example of advanced interaction in AJAX could be a login form that sends user credentials to the server via an AJAX call, without having to reload the entire page. This way, the user can access their account quickly and seamlessly. Here is an example of code to achieve this functionality:

```html
<!DOCTYPE html>
<html>
<head>
    <title>Login Form</title>
    <script src="https://ajax.googleapis.com/ajax/libs/jquery/3.5.1/jquery.min.js"></script>
</head>
<body>

<form id="loginForm" action="login.php"
```

```html
  method="post">
    <input type="text" name="username" placeholder="Username">
    <input type="password" name="password" placeholder="Password">
    <button type="submit">Login</button>
</form>

<div id="message"></div>

<script>
```
```javascript
$(document).ready(function(){
    $('#loginForm').submit(function(e){
        e.preventDefault();
        var formData = $(this).serialize();

        $.ajax({
            type: 'POST',
```

```
            url: $(this).attr('action'),

            data: formData,

            success: function(response){

                $('#message').text(response);

            }
        });
      });
});
</script>


</body>
</html>
```

In this example, the login form sends the user-entered data to the server via an AJAX call to the `login.php` file. The server receives the data, verifies the user credentials, and returns a confirmation or error message, which is displayed in the `#message` element without reloading the page.

Another example of advanced interaction in AJAX could be a search form that shows search results in real-time as the user types. This can be achieved using the debouncing technique to avoid too frequent and heavy AJAX calls to the server. Here is an example of code to achieve this functionality:

```html
<!DOCTYPE html>
<html>
<head>
    <title>Real-Time Search</title>
    <script src="https://ajax.googleapis.com/ajax/libs/jquery/3.5.1/jquery.min.js"></script>
</head>
```

```html
<body>

<input type="text" id="searchInput" placeholder="Search...">
<ul id="searchResults"></ul>

<script>
$(document).ready(function(){
    var typingTimer;
    var doneTypingInterval = 500;
    var $searchInput = $('#searchInput');
    var $searchResults = $('#searchResults');

    $searchInput.keyup(function(){
        clearTimeout(typingTimer);

        if ($searchInput.val()) {
```

```javascript
typingTimer = setTimeout(function(){
    var query = $searchInput.val();

    $.ajax({
        type: 'GET',
        url: 'search.php',
        data: {query: query},
        success: function(response){
            $searchResults.empty();

            if (response.length > 0) {

                response.forEach(function(result){

                    $searchResults.append('<li>' + result + '</li>');

                });
            } else {
```

```
$searchResults.append('<li>No results found</li>');
                }
            }
        });
    }, doneTypingInterval);
  }
 });
});
</script>


</body>
</html>
```

In this example, the user can type in the search box and the search results are displayed in real-time as unordered lists. An AJAX call is made every time the user stops typing for a specified time interval to avoid too frequent server calls.

Advanced interactions in AJAX allow the creation of more sophisticated and user-friendly web applications, offering a richer and more dynamic user experience. By efficiently utilizing AJAX, website performance can be improved and user interaction can be made more intuitive and immediate.

To fully leverage the potential of AJAX, it is important to design and implement interactions carefully, considering user needs and ensuring optimal page performance. With a thoughtful approach and proper implementation, advanced interactions in AJAX can transform a website into an interactive and engaging experience for users.

5. Callback, XMLHttpRequest, asynchronous in Ajax

When we talk about Ajax, we refer to the use of technologies like XMLHttpRequest (XHR) to send and receive data from a server without having to reload the entire web page. In particular, the asynchronous aspect of Ajax is what allows performing operations on the server without interrupting the user experience on the client side.

A key element in using Ajax is handling callbacks. Callbacks are simply functions that are passed as arguments to other functions and are called when an asynchronous operation is completed. This is crucial because Ajax requests can take time to complete, so it is important to be able to handle the response once it is ready.

For example, let's say we want to retrieve data from a remote server using an

XMLHttpRequest request. We can define a function to handle the server's response through a callback. Here is an example of how it could be implemented:

```javascript
function fetchData(url, callback) {

  var xhr = new XMLHttpRequest();

  xhr.onreadystatechange = function() {
    if (xhr.readyState === 4 && xhr.status === 200) {
      callback(xhr.responseText);
    }
  };

  xhr.open('GET', url, true);
  xhr.send();
}
```

```
function handleData(response) {
  console.log(response);
}


fetchData('http://example.com/data', handleData);
```

In this example, the `fetchData` function receives a URL from which to retrieve data and a callback function `handleData`. When the XHR request is successfully completed (readyState = 4 and status = 200), the `handleData` callback is called, receiving the server's response as a parameter.

The use of callbacks is essential in Ajax to efficiently handle the server's response and update the web page with the obtained data. Without them, it would be challenging to synchronously coordinate the request and the server's response.

Furthermore, the concept of asynchrony is what allows Ajax to be so powerful. XHR requests are executed asynchronously, allowing the browser to continue performing other operations while the request is waiting for a response from the server. This eliminates the need to reload the entire page and enables users to update only the specific parts of the web page that are necessary.

Asynchrony in Ajax is primarily handled through the `async` attribute in XHR objects. When set to `true`, the XHR request is executed asynchronously, allowing the browser to continue executing JavaScript code without waiting for the server response. By default, the `async` attribute is set to `true`.

```javascript
```

xhr.open('GET', url, true); // asynchronous
```

However, it is important to note that asynchrony can lead to state management issues in complex applications. Therefore, it is important to handle callbacks correctly and monitor the request's state to ensure consistent behavior and prevent bugs.

Callbacks, XMLHttpRequest requests, and asynchrony are fundamental elements in Ajax that enable the creation of interactive and responsive web applications. Properly managing these concepts is essential to fully harness the potential of Ajax and enhance the user experience on the web.
```

6. Examples of Callback, XMLHttpRequest, asynchronous in Ajax

1. Callback:

```javascript
function fetchData(url, callback) {
  fetch(url)
    .then(response => response.json())
    .then(data => {
      callback(data);
    })
    .catch(error => console.error('Error:', error));
}

function displayData(data) {
  console.log(data);
}
```

```javascript
fetchData('https://jsonplaceholder.typicode.com/users', displayData);
```

2. XMLHttpRequest:

```javascript
var xhttp = new XMLHttpRequest();
xhttp.onreadystatechange = function() {
  if (this.readyState == 4 && this.status == 200) {
    console.log(this.responseText);
  }
};
xhttp.open("GET", "https://jsonplaceholder.typicode.com/users", true);
xhttp.send();
```

3. Asynchronous in Ajax:

```javascript
$.ajax({
  url: 'https://jsonplaceholder.typicode.com/users',
  method: 'GET',
  success: function(data) {
    console.log(data);
  },
  error: function(xhr, status, error) {
    console.error('Error:', error);
  }
});
```

7. Event Management in Ajax

Event management in Ajax is crucial for interacting with elements on a web page asynchronously, without reloading the entire page. Events in Ajax can be triggered by various user actions, such as clicking a button, submitting a form, hovering over an element, etc. This allows for updating only the portions of the page affected by the change, improving user experience and optimizing site performance.

To handle events in Ajax, one must use the `addEventListener` function to capture the desired event and associate it with a function that will execute the Ajax call. Let's look at a practical example of handling a click on a button to make an Ajax call and update a part of the page with the result obtained.

Let's say we have a button with the id "btn-ajax" and a div element with the id "result" where we want to display the result of the Ajax call. Here's how the HTML code could look:

```html
<button id="btn-ajax">Click to make an Ajax call</button>

<div id="result"></div>
```

To handle the click on the button and make the Ajax call, we can write some JavaScript code using the jQuery library, which simplifies event handling and Ajax calls. Here's an example of what the code could look like:

```javascript
$(document).ready(function() {

  $('#btn-ajax').on('click', function() {
```

```
      $.ajax({
        url: 'url_of_the_ajax_call',
        method: 'GET',
        success: function(response) {
          $('#result').html(response);
        },
        error: function(xhr, status, error) {
          console.log('Error during the Ajax call');
        }
      });
    });
});
```

In this code, we used jQuery to handle the click on the button with the id "btn-ajax". When the event is triggered, a GET Ajax call is made to the specified URL. If the call is successful, the obtained result is inserted inside the div element with the id "result", otherwise an error message is displayed on the console.

This is just a simple example of handling an event in Ajax with jQuery, but the possibilities are endless. We can use Ajax to dynamically update a form, load data from a remote server, manage drag and drop of elements, and much more. The key to proper event management in Ajax is understanding how event listening works and how to efficiently execute Ajax calls.

8. Error Handling in Ajax

Error handling in Ajax is a crucial aspect to consider when developing a web application that relies on asynchronous requests to the server. When using Ajax to send and receive data to and from the server, it is important to take into account the potential errors that can occur during this process.

There are several types of errors that you may encounter during an Ajax call, such as network errors, HTTP errors, syntax errors in received data, and so on. It is essential to have an effective strategy to handle these errors in order to provide a better user experience and facilitate debugging and code maintenance.

One of the most common practices in handling errors in Ajax is using specific callbacks to handle the success and error of requests. For example, the XMLHttpRequest object in JavaScript provides two main callbacks to handle the response of the request: onload to handle success and onerror to handle errors.

```javascript
var xhr = new XMLHttpRequest();

xhr.open('GET', 'https://api.example.com/data', true);


xhr.onload = function() {
  if (xhr.status >= 200 && xhr.status < 300) {
    // Gestione della risposta di successo
    var data = JSON.parse(xhr.responseText);
    console.log(data);
  } else {
    // Gestione degli errori HTTP
    console.error('Errore durante la richiesta: ' + xhr.status);
  }
};
```

```
xhr.onerror = function() {

  // Gestione degli errori di rete

  console.error('Errore di rete durante la richiesta');

};


xhr.send();
```

In the example above, the onload function is called when the request is successful and returns a response with an HTTP status code between 200 and 299. In case of HTTP errors, the onerror function is called instead.

```
var xhr = new XMLHttpRequest();

xhr.open('GET', 'https://api.example.com/data', true);


xhr.onload = function() {

  if (xhr.status >= 200 && xhr.status < 300) {

    try {
```

```javascript
      var data = JSON.parse(xhr.responseText);

      console.log(data);

    } catch (e) {

      // Gestione dell'errore di parsing dei dati

      console.error('Errore durante il parsing dei dati: ' + e.message);

    }

  } else {

    console.error('Errore durante la richiesta: ' + xhr.status);

  }
};


xhr.onerror = function() {

  console.error('Errore di rete durante la richiesta');

};
```

xhr.send();

In addition to handling HTTP and network errors, it is also important to handle any errors in parsing received data. For example, if you are expecting a JSON object as a response and the server sends an invalid string, it is crucial to handle this error so as not to interrupt the script execution.

In addition to using specific callbacks to handle errors in Ajax requests, it is also advisable to implement a centralized error handling system to simplify error management throughout the application. For example, you could create a utility that automatically handles errors and displays meaningful error messages to the user.

function handleError(error) {

  console.error('Si è verificato un errore:', error);

  // Mostra un messaggio di errore all'utente

  alert('Si è verificato un errore durante la

richiesta, ti preghiamo di riprovare più tardi.');

}

```javascript
var xhr = new XMLHttpRequest();
xhr.open('GET', 'https://api.example.com/data', true);

xhr.onload = function() {
  if (xhr.status >= 200 && xhr.status < 300) {
    try {
      var data = JSON.parse(xhr.responseText);
      console.log(data);
    } catch (e) {
      handleError(e);
    }
  } else {
    handleError('Errore durante la richiesta: ' + xhr.status);
```

        }
    };

xhr.onerror = function() {

  handleError('Errore di rete durante la richiesta');

};

xhr.send();

This way, you can more efficiently and consistently handle errors throughout the application without having to repeat the same error handling logic in every Ajax request.

In conclusion, error handling in Ajax is a fundamental aspect to consider when developing a web application that relies on asynchronous requests to the server. By using specific callbacks to handle errors, managing HTTP, network, and data parsing errors, and implementing a centralized error handling system, you can improve the user experience and simplify code maintenance.

9. Cross-browser compatibility in Ajax

Cross-browser compatibility in Ajax is a fundamental concept in the design and development of websites that utilize Ajax (Asynchronous JavaScript and XML) technologies to interact with the server asynchronously without having to reload the entire page. The goal of cross-browser compatibility is to ensure that JavaScript code functions correctly on all major web browsers, such as Chrome, Firefox, Safari, Edge, and Internet Explorer, without causing errors or unexpected behaviors.

To ensure that Ajax code works properly on different browsers, it is essential to follow some best practices and programming techniques. One of the first things to do is to make sure to use a solid and well-supported Ajax framework, such as jQuery or Axios, which automatically handles differences between browsers and provides consistent syntax for making Ajax requests.

Another important practice is to test the code on different browsers and versions to verify that it works correctly everywhere. It is important to take into account implementation differences between browsers, such as variations in event handling, support for modern APIs, and differences in JavaScript syntax. An example of cross-browser compatibility in Ajax could be the following:

```javascript
function fetchData(url, callback) {
  var xhr = new XMLHttpRequest();
  xhr.open('GET', url, true);
  xhr.onreadystatechange = function() {
    if(xhr.readyState === 4 && xhr.status === 200) {
      callback(xhr.responseText);
    }
```

```
  };

  xhr.send();

}


fetchData('https://api.example.com/data', function(response) {

  console.log(response);

});
```

In this example, the `fetchData` function makes an asynchronous GET request using the browser's native `XMLHttpRequest` object to fetch data from a remote API. The `callback` parameter is a function that will be called when the request is successfully completed, returning the request result as text.

This is a basic technique for making Ajax requests without the use of a framework like jQuery, but it is important to note that it needs to be handled differently for older browsers like Internet Explorer 6-8, which may require the use of ActiveX or other alternative solutions.

For better cross-browser compatibility, it is advisable to use a library like jQuery that automatically handles implementation differences between browsers and provides a simpler and more consistent interface for making Ajax requests. For example, using jQuery, the above code could be rewritten more compactly as follows:

```javascript
$.ajax({
  url: 'https://api.example.com/data',
  success: function(response) {
    console.log(response);
  }
});
```

This `$.ajax` call from jQuery will automatically handle the difference between browsers and provide a simpler interface for making Ajax requests, ensuring greater compatibility and ease of maintenance in the long term.

In conclusion, cross-browser compatibility in Ajax is crucial to ensure that JavaScript code functions correctly on all major web browsers, avoiding errors and unexpected behaviors. Following best practices and using established libraries like jQuery can greatly simplify the development process and ensure better cross-browser compatibility for modern web applications.

10. Methods in AJAX

There are several methods and techniques that can be used with Ajax to achieve desired results.

1. GET Method:

The HTTP GET method is used to retrieve data from a server. This method is very common with Ajax because it allows you to get information without having to send complex parameters. For example, if you want to retrieve a user's data from a database, you can use the GET method to request the data from the server and display it on the page without having to reload the entire page.

Example of using the GET method in Ajax:

```javascript
$.ajax({
```

```
    url: "get_user_data.php",
    type: "GET",
    success: function(response) {
      console.log(response);
    },
    error: function(err) {
      console.log(err);
    }
});
```

2. POST Method:

The HTTP POST method is used to send data to a server for processing. This method is useful when you need to send sensitive or complex data to the server. For example, if you want to send order details to the server, you can use the POST method to send the data and update the database without having to reload the page.

Example of using the POST method in Ajax:

```javascript
$.ajax({
  url: "submit_order.php",
  type: "POST",
  data: {
    item: "iPhone",
    quantity: 1,
    total: 999.99
  },
  success: function(response) {
    console.log(response);
  },
  error: function(err) {
    console.log(err);
```

    }
});
```

### 3. PUT Method:

The HTTP PUT method is used to update existing resources or create new resources on the server. This method is useful when you want to modify existing data without sending a new complete record. For example, if you want to update a user's name in the database, you can use the PUT method to update the existing record without sending all the data again.

Example of using the PUT method in Ajax:

```javascript
$.ajax({
  url: "update_user.php",

```
  type: "PUT",
  data: {
    id: 123,
    name: "Alice"
  },
  success: function(response) {
    console.log(response);
  },
  error: function(err) {
    console.log(err);
  }
});
```

4. DELETE Method:

The HTTP DELETE method is used to delete resources from the server. This method is useful when you want to delete an existing record in the database without sending a separate request. For example, if you want to delete a comment from a post, you can use the DELETE method to remove the comment without having to reload the page.

Example of using the DELETE method in Ajax:

```javascript
$.ajax({
  url: "delete_comment.php",
  type: "DELETE",
  data: {
    id: 456
  },
  success: function(response) {
    console.log(response);
  },
```

```
    error: function(err) {

        console.log(err);

    }
});
```

These are just some examples of methods that can be used with Ajax to create interactive and dynamic web applications. It is important to know the various methods available and how to use them properly to achieve the desired results. Combining these methods with Ajax allows you to create smooth and responsive user experiences without having to reload the entire web page.

11. Parameters in AJAX

AJAX allows for making asynchronous requests to a web server without having to reload the entire page. This allows for updating a specific portion of the page without interrupting the user's experience. Parameters play a crucial role in AJAX as they allow for sending data to the server and receiving a response dynamically.

Parameters in AJAX can be passed through different methods, such as query strings, JSON objects, or form data. Below, we will see some examples of how to use parameters in AJAX to make requests to a server.

1. Query string:

The query string is a string of parameters that is added to the AJAX request URL. These parameters are separated by the "?" symbol and separated from each other by the "&"

symbol. For example:

```
var parameter1 = 'value1';
var parameter2 = 'value2';

var xhr = new XMLHttpRequest();
xhr.open('GET', 'http://www.example.com/api?parameter1=' + parameter1 + '&parameter2=' + parameter2, true);
xhr.send();
```

In this case, the parameters "parameter1" and "parameter2" are passed to the server through the query string.

2. JSON object:

Another way to pass parameters in AJAX is to use a JSON object. This method is particularly useful when there are many parameters to send to the server. For example:

```
var parameters = {
  parameter1: 'value1',
  parameter2: 'value2'
};

var xhr = new XMLHttpRequest();
xhr.open('POST', 'http://www.example.com/api', true);
xhr.setRequestHeader('Content-Type', 'application/json');
xhr.send(JSON.stringify(parameters));
```

In this case, the parameters are placed inside a JSON object and then sent to the server using the POST method.

3. Form data:

Lastly, you can use the FormData method to pass parameters in AJAX when sending data from an HTML form. For example:

```
var form = document.getElementById('myForm');

var formData = new FormData(form);


var xhr = new XMLHttpRequest();

xhr.open('POST', 'http://www.example.com/api', true);

xhr.send(formData);
```

In this case, all the data from the HTML form is collected by the FormData object and sent to the server using the POST method.

Parameters are essential in AJAX to dynamically send and receive data from a server. It is important to choose the most suitable method based on the needs of your project and ensure that the parameters are correctly formatted to be interpreted by the server.

12. Implementation of Ajax in JavaScript

The implementation of AJAX in JavaScript and XML, in JavaScript, is crucial for creating dynamic and interactive web applications. Thanks to this technology, it is possible to exchange data with the server asynchronously, without having to reload the entire page. This allows users to interact with the site more smoothly and quickly, thus improving the user experience.

To use AJAX in JavaScript, it is necessary to first create an XMLHttpRequest object, which handles HTTP requests asynchronously. This object allows you to send requests to the server and handle responses dynamically. Below is an example of how to create an XMLHttpRequest object:

```javascript
var xhr = new XMLHttpRequest();
```

```

Once the XMLHttpRequest object is created, it can be used to send requests to the server and handle responses. For example, to make a GET request to the server and retrieve the returned data, the following code can be used:

```javascript
xhr.open('GET', 'https://api.example.com/data', true);

xhr.onreadystatechange = function() {

    if (xhr.readyState == 4 && xhr.status == 200) {

        var data = JSON.parse(xhr.responseText);

        console.log(data);

    }

};

xhr.send();
```
```

```

In this example, a GET request is made to the server at 'https://api.example.com/data' asynchronously. When the request is successfully completed (readyState = 4 and status = 200), the data returned by the server is converted from JSON to a JavaScript object and printed to the browser console.

In addition to GET requests, it is also possible to make POST requests using AJAX. For example, to send data to the server through a POST request, the following code can be used:

```javascript
var data = { username: 'example', password: 'password' };

xhr.open('POST', 'https://api.example.com/login', true);

```
xhr.setRequestHeader('Content-Type', 'application/json');

xhr.onreadystatechange = function() {

    if (xhr.readyState == 4 && xhr.status == 200) {

        var response = JSON.parse(xhr.responseText);

        console.log(response);

    }

};

xhr.send(JSON.stringify(data));
```

In this case, a POST request is sent to the server at 'https://api.example.com/login' with the user data (username and password) as the request body. Once the request is successfully completed, the server's response is converted from JSON to a JavaScript object and printed to the browser console.

To handle any errors during AJAX requests, the onerror event of the XMLHttpRequest object can be used. For example, to handle an error during a request to the server, the following code can be used:

```javascript
xhr.onerror = function() {
    console.error('Error during request to the server');
};
```

In this way, the error event during a request to the server is handled and an error message is printed on the browser console.

Furthermore, AJAX can be used to dynamically update the content of a web page without having to reload the entire page. For example, displaying a list of blog posts without reloading the page:

```javascript
var xhr = new XMLHttpRequest();

xhr.open('GET', 'https://api.example.com/posts', true);

xhr.onreadystatechange = function() {

    if (xhr.readyState == 4 && xhr.status == 200) {

        var posts = JSON.parse(xhr.responseText);

        var postsContainer = document.getElementById('posts-container');

        posts.forEach(function(post) {

            var postElement = document.createElement('div');

            postElement.textContent = post.title;
```

```
      postsContainer.appendChild(postElement);
    });
  }
};
xhr.send();
```

In this example, a GET request is made to the server to retrieve the list of blog posts. Once the data is obtained, HTML elements are created to display the posts within a container on the web page.

Implementing AJAX in JavaScript is essential for creating dynamic and interactive web applications. By using AJAX, it is possible to make requests to the server asynchronously and handle the responses dynamically, thus improving the user experience on the site.

13. Using jQuery to simplify the implementation of Ajax

jQuery is a very popular JavaScript library that greatly simplifies the implementation of Ajax in web applications. Thanks to its ease of use and power, jQuery has become an essential tool for many web developers.

One of jQuery's main features is its ability to simplify the handling of Ajax requests, which would otherwise be very complex and laborious to implement manually. With jQuery, you can make an Ajax request in just a few lines of code, without having to manually handle the various stages of the request (such as creating an XMLHttpRequest object, handling loading events, etc.).

To use jQuery to make an Ajax request, you simply call the $.ajax() method passing a configuration object that specifies the details of the request as an argument. For example, the following code makes a simple Ajax request to retrieve data from a server:

```javascript
$.ajax({
    url: "https://api.example.com/data",
    method: "GET",
    success: function(response) {
        console.log("Data received:", response);
    },
    error: function(xhr, status, error) {
        console.error("An error occurred:", error);
    }
});
```

In this example, the $.ajax() method is called

with a configuration object containing three main keys: url, method, and success. The url key specifies the URL of the server to contact, the method key specifies the type of HTTP request to make (in this case GET) and the success key specifies the function to execute when the request is successful. In this case, the success function simply prints the data received from the request on the console.

Furthermore, you can specify other options in the Ajax request configuration, such as the expected data type (dataType), parameters to pass with the request (data), any headers to send (headers), and so on.

Another powerful feature of jQuery is the ability to make Ajax requests asynchronously, so that the web page does not freeze during data loading from the server. This is crucial to ensure a good user experience, especially in modern web applications that have to handle large amounts of real-time data.

Finally, jQuery also offers a series of utility methods to further simplify the implementation of Ajax functionality. For example, the $.get() method allows you to make a simple GET request, the $.post() method allows you to make a simple POST request, and so on.

In conclusion, using jQuery to simplify the implementation of Ajax in web applications is extremely useful and convenient. Thanks to its ease of use, power, and flexibility, jQuery makes it easy to handle Ajax requests, improving the interactivity and performance of web applications.

14. Using front-end frameworks to handle Ajax calls

A front-end framework is a set of tools and libraries that simplify the development of interactive and dynamic user interfaces. One of the most common tasks for a web application is to make Ajax calls to retrieve or send data to the server asynchronously, without having to reload the entire page.

There are different front-end frameworks that offer features to handle Ajax calls in a simple and efficient way. Some of the most popular ones include jQuery, Angular, React, and Vue.js. In this article, we will focus on using jQuery to handle Ajax calls.

jQuery is a lightweight and powerful JavaScript library that simplifies DOM manipulation, adds animations, event handling, and, precisely, Ajax calls. To use jQuery to make an Ajax call, you simply need to use the $.ajax() method.

Here's an example of how to use jQuery to make an Ajax call:

```javascript
$.ajax({
  url: "https://api.example.com/data",
  type: "GET",
  success: function(data) {
    console.log("Data received:", data);
  },
  error: function(xhr, status, error) {
    console.error("Error in request:", error);
  }
});
```

In this example, we are making a GET request to the URL "https://api.example.com/data". When the call is successful, the callback function passed to success() will be executed, and the data received from the server will be printed on the console. If an error occurs during the call, the callback function passed to error() will be executed, and the error will be printed on the console.

jQuery offers many options to customize Ajax calls, such as setting custom headers, using methods other than GET and POST, managing authentication, and handling sent or received data.

For example, to send data to the server in a POST request, we can use the following code:

```javascript
$.ajax({
```

```
    url: "https://api.example.com/data",
    type: "POST",
    data: { name: "Mario", lastname: "Rossi" },
    success: function(data) {
        console.log("Data saved successfully:", data);
    },
    error: function(xhr, status, error) {
        console.error("Error in request:", error);
    }
});
```

In this case, we are sending the data { name: "Mario", lastname: "Rossi" } to the server using a POST request to the URL "https://api.example.com/data". When the call is successful, the data returned by the server will be printed on the console.

jQuery also provides the $.get() and $.post() methods to make GET and POST requests more concise. For example, to get data from the URL "https://api.example.com/data" using the GET method, we can write:

```javascript
$.get("https://api.example.com/data", function(data) {
  console.log("Data received:", data);
});
```

In this example, we are using the $.get() method to make a GET request to the URL "https://api.example.com/data". When the call is successful, the data received from the server will be printed on the console.

Using a front-end framework like jQuery to handle Ajax calls makes the code more concise, readable, and maintainable. jQuery greatly simplifies the management of Ajax calls, allowing developers to focus on the application's functionalities rather than HTTP request handling. With jQuery, it is possible to make Ajax calls efficiently and easily manage the data sent and received from the server.

15. Parameters in AJAX

When it comes to AJAX (Asynchronous JavaScript and XML), parameters are a fundamental element of every request that is sent to the server. Parameters allow passing information to the server to specify which resource should be retrieved or which action should be executed.

There are several ways to pass parameters in an AJAX request. The most common method is to use the "data" property of the request configuration object. For example, if you want to send a parameter named "name" with the value "Mario", you can do it like this:

```javascript
$.ajax({
  url: 'http://example.com/api',
  method: 'GET',
```

```
    data: {name: 'Mario'},

    success: function(response) {

      console.log(response);

    }
  });
```
```

In this example, the parameter "name" with the value "Mario" is passed to the server as part of the request. The server can then use this parameter to process the request based on the information provided.

It is also possible to pass parameters through the request URL using the GET method. For example, if you want to send the same parameter "name" with the value "Mario" but this time through the URL, you can do it like this:
```

```javascript
$.ajax({
  url: 'http://example.com/api?name=Mario',
  method: 'GET',
  success: function(response) {
    console.log(response);
  }
});
```

In this case, the parameter "name" with the value "Mario" is passed directly in the request URL. The server can still extract this parameter to process the request based on the information provided.

Another option is to pass parameters using the POST method. This method is often used when transmitting large amounts of data or sensitive information that should not be visible in the request URL. Here is an example:

```javascript
$.ajax({
  url: 'http://example.com/api',
  method: 'POST',
  data: {name: 'Mario'},
  success: function(response) {
    console.log(response);
  }
});
```

In this case, the parameter "name" with the value "Mario" is passed as part of the body of the POST request. This ensures that the data is hidden from the URL and not visible to potential attackers.

In general, it is important to be cautious about the parameters being passed in an AJAX request. Parameters may contain sensitive information or be used to perform specific actions on the server. Always make sure to validate and sanitize the parameters to prevent attacks like SQL injection or cross-site scripting.

In conclusion, parameters are a key element of AJAX requests and allow passing information to the server to specify which resource should be retrieved or which action should be executed. There are several ways to pass parameters, including using the "data" property of the request configuration object, passing parameters through the request URL, or using the POST method. It is important to be careful about the parameters being passed and ensure to validate and sanitize the data to prevent potential attacks.

16. Monitoring AJAX with PHP

Monitoring AJAX with PHP is a crucial aspect of tracking a web application's performance and functionality. AJAX, short for Asynchronous JavaScript and XML, enables web pages to update content dynamically without necessitating a full page refresh. While this enhances user experience, it also presents challenges in monitoring and overseeing AJAX requests.

A common approach to monitoring AJAX requests in PHP involves utilizing tools like Xdebug or Firebug. These tools empower developers to examine AJAX requests and responses, assess performance metrics, and troubleshoot any potential problems during AJAX communication.

Apart from external tools, developers can integrate customized monitoring systems within their PHP code. For instance, developers can log AJAX requests to a database or text file for later assessment. This can offer insights into the frequency of AJAX requests, response times, and potential bottlenecks in the application.

Below is an example demonstrating how to monitor AJAX requests in PHP using a basic logging system:

[PHP code example provided]

```php
// Start by creating a function to log AJAX requests
function logAjaxRequest($url, $method, $data) {

    $logFile = 'ajax_logs.txt';

    $logData = date('Y-m-d H:i:s') . ' - ' . $url . ' - ' . $method . ' - ' . json_encode($data) . PHP_EOL;


    file_put_contents($logFile, $logData,
```

```php
    FILE_APPEND);
}


// Next, handle the AJAX request and call the logAjaxRequest function
if (!empty($_SERVER['HTTP_X_REQUESTED_WITH']) && strtolower($_SERVER['HTTP_X_REQUESTED_WITH']) == 'xmlhttprequest') {
    $url = $_POST['url'];
    $method = $_POST['method'];
    $data = $_POST['data'];

    // Perform the AJAX request using cURL or another HTTP client
    // For demonstration purposes, we'll just log the request data
    logAjaxRequest($url, $method, $data);
}
```

In this example, a function called logAjaxRequest is created to log the URL,

method, and data of an AJAX request to a text file named 'ajax_logs.txt', alongside a timestamp for reference. The script then ensures that the request is an AJAX request, extracts the necessary information, and calls the logAjaxRequest function.

It is important to note that this example serves as a fundamental illustration of monitoring AJAX requests in PHP. In reality, developers might want to implement more sophisticated logging, error handling, and analytics to gain deeper insights into the performance of their AJAX requests.

Furthermore, developers can leverage PHP frameworks and libraries offering built-in tools for AJAX request monitoring, such as Laravel's AJAX debugging tools or Symfony's Profiler component.

In essence, monitoring AJAX requests in PHP is paramount for sustaining a high-performing and reliable web application. Through effective monitoring and logging systems, developers can understand the performance and behavior of their AJAX requests, enabling them to detect and address potential issues promptly.

17. Monitoring AJAX with ASP.NET Data submission (GET and POST)

To monitor AJAX calls with ASP.NET, it is important to understand how to send data using both the GET and POST methods.

First of all, you can monitor AJAX calls using browser development tools, such as Chrome or Firefox developer console. These tools allow you to view all calls made by the web page, including details of AJAX requests like sent parameters and received responses.

To send data using the GET method, you can use the $.ajax function of jQuery. For example, the following code sends an AJAX request using the GET method and displays the received response:

```javascript
```

```
$.ajax({
    url: 'page.php',
    type: 'GET',
    data: { parameter1: 'value1', parameter2: 'value2' },
    success: function(response) {
        console.log(response);
    },
    error: function(xhr, status, error) {
        console.log(error);
    }
});
```

In this example, the parameters sent to page.php are specified in the data object and the received response is displayed in the browser console.

To send data using the POST method, you can use the same approach, changing the request type from GET to POST. For example, the following code sends an AJAX request using the POST method and displays the received response:

```javascript
$.ajax({
    url: 'page.php',
    type: 'POST',
    data: { parameter1: 'value1', parameter2: 'value2' },
    success: function(response) {
        console.log(response);
    },
    error: function(xhr, status, error) {
        console.log(error);
    }
```

});
```

Again, the parameters to be sent are specified in the data object and the received response is displayed in the browser console.

To monitor AJAX data submission in ASP.NET, you can use the PageMethods function provided by ASP.NET WebForms. This function allows you to create methods in .aspx.cs files that can be called through AJAX requests. For example, the following code demonstrates how to define a method in an ASP.NET WebForm page and invoke it through an AJAX request:

```c#
namespace TestWebApp
{
    public partial class _Default :
```
```

```
System.Web.UI.Page
    {
        [System.Web.Services.WebMethod]
        public static string ExampleMethod(string parameter1, string parameter2)
        {
            return "Parameter 1 is " + parameter1 + " and parameter 2 is " + parameter2;
        }
    }
}
```

In the .aspx file, you can invoke the ExampleMethod using the PageMethods function in JavaScript:

```javascript
```

```
function sendData() {

    var parameter1 = 'value1';

    var parameter2 = 'value2';


    PageMethods.ExampleMethod(parameter1, parameter2, function(response) {

        console.log(response);

    });
}
```

When the sendData function is called, the ExampleMethod defined in the ASP.NET WebForm page is invoked and the response is displayed in the browser console.

Monitoring AJAX calls with ASP.NET is essential to better understand and manage interactions between the frontend and backend of the website. Knowing how to send data using the GET and POST methods, along with the ability to monitor AJAX calls, is crucial for the development of dynamic and efficient web applications.

18. Ajax customer database

With the use of AJAX, we can achieve a smoother and more responsive user experience, eliminating the need to wait for the loading of a new page every time we want to view or update data.

A practical example of using AJAX could be loading a list of customers within a table from a database. By using AJAX, we can asynchronously retrieve customer data and update the table without refreshing the entire page. This way, the user can quickly and seamlessly view the list of customers.

But in order to use AJAX and display customer data, it is necessary to have a complete customer database. The customer database is a set of detailed information about a company's customers, which can include personal data such as name, surname, address, phone number, email, as well as commercial information like customer type, purchase history, preferences, etc.

To maintain a complete and updated customer database, it is important to gather and store all customer information in a database. This database should be efficiently designed to easily manage data update and retrieval requests through AJAX.

For example, let's suppose a company that sells products online and wants to maintain a customer database to offer personalized and efficient service. In this case, the company could create a database containing the following customer information:

- Name and surname

- Address

- Phone number

- Email

- Purchase history

- Purchase preferences

Using AJAX, the company could create a web page where the user can enter their name and surname to search for information related to their customer profile. When the user enters the data and clicks the search button, the page sends a request to the server which responds with the corresponding customer data.

Thanks to the use of AJAX, updating customer data is quick and uninterrupted, allowing the company to offer better and more efficient service to its customers. In the context of a customer database management application with code, the use of AJAX can be very useful for allowing the user to view, insert, modify, and delete customer information without having to reload the page each time. For example, imagine having a table that displays customer data (name, surname, email, phone, etc.) and an "Add customer" button that allows the user to add a new customer.

When the user clicks the "Add customer" button, instead of reloading the page to display a new insertion form, we can use AJAX to send a request to the server and obtain an insertion form in dialog mode, without disrupting the user's browsing on the main page.

For example, we can use jQuery to efficiently handle AJAX calls:

```javascript
$('#add-customer').click(function() {
  $.ajax({
    url: 'insert_customer.php',
    type: 'GET',
    success: function(data) {
```

```js
        $('#dialog-insert-customer').html(data).dialog('open');
      }
    });
  });

  $('#dialog-insert-customer').dialog({
    autoOpen: false,
    modal: true,
    buttons: {
      "Save": function() {
        $.ajax({
          url: 'save_customer.php',
          type: 'POST',
          data: $('#customer-form').serialize(),
          success: function() {
            // Update the customer table without reloading the page
```

```
        }
    });
    $(this).dialog('close');
  }
 }
});
```
```

In this example, when the user clicks on the "Add Customer" button, a GET request is sent to the server to retrieve the customer data entry form to be inserted in the dialog with ID "dialog-ins-customer". Once the data is entered and "Save" is clicked, the data is sent via a POST request to the server to save the new customer in the database.

Another common use case of AJAX in customer records is real-time data search and display without having to reload the entire page. For example, we can have a search field that allows the user to search for a specific
```

customer by their name or surname.

```javascript
$('#ricerca-cliente').keyup(function() {
  var query = $(this).val();

  $.ajax({
    url: 'ricerca_cliente.php',
    type: 'GET',
    data: { query: query },
    success: function(data) {
      $('#tabella-clienti').html(data);
    }
  });
});
```

In this example, whenever the user types something in the search field, a GET request is sent to the server to search for customers that match the entered query. The results are then displayed in the customer's table without having to reload the page.

Using AJAX in customer records with code can greatly improve the usability and efficiency of the application, allowing users to interact with data more quickly and intuitively. However, it is important to properly manage AJAX calls and ensure the security of operations to avoid vulnerabilities or system errors.

In conclusion, AJAX and a well-structured customer registry are essential elements to create a positive user experience and effectively manage customer information for a company. By using these technologies correctly, it is possible to improve communication and relationships with customers, offering them personalized and quality service.

19. AJAX User Side and Server Side

AJAX is a web development technique that allows for sending and receiving data asynchronously between the user side and the server side without the need to reload the entire page. This enables the creation of smoother and more dynamic user experiences without interruptions.

On the user side, AJAX is commonly used to make HTTP calls to a server to retrieve or send data without refreshing the entire web page. An example is using AJAX to make a GET request to retrieve new messages from a real-time chat without needing to update the complete web page.

An example of JavaScript code for making an AJAX call using jQuery:

```javascript
```

```
$.ajax({
  type: "GET",
  url: "https://api.example.com/messages",
  success: function(data) {
    // handle server response
    console.log(data);
  },
  error: function(xhr, status, error) {
    // handle any errors
    console.error(error);
  }
});
```

In this example, a GET request is made to the URL "https://api.example.com/messages" and the server response is handled in the success function. Errors during the request are handled in the error function.

On the server side, it is important to handle AJAX calls by creating specific routes or endpoints to receive and process requests. For instance, you can create a RESTful API that accepts AJAX requests to retrieve or send data.

Example PHP code to handle an AJAX request and return a JSON response:

```php
<?php
// Check the request method
if ($_SERVER['REQUEST_METHOD'] === 'GET') {
  // Process the request
  $messages = [
    ['id' => 1, 'text' => 'Hello!'],
    ['id' => 2, 'text' => 'How are you?']
```

```
    ];

    // Return data in JSON format
    header('Content-Type: application/json');
    echo json_encode($messages);
}
?>
```

In this example, a route is created to handle an AJAX GET request and return an array of messages in JSON format. These data will be processed by the JavaScript callback function in the AJAX call's success function.

AJAX is a powerful web development technique that allows for creating dynamic interactions between the user side and the server side without interruptions. By using AJAX alongside JavaScript and server-side technologies like PHP, you can develop richer and more interactive user experiences on the web.

20. Security and Analysis in Ajax

Thanks to Ajax, it is possible to send and receive data from the server in the background, without interrupting the user experience. However, due to its asynchronous nature, the use of Ajax can pose risks to the security of web applications.

One of the main risks associated with the use of Ajax is the possibility of Cross-Site Scripting (XSS) attacks. This type of attack occurs when a malicious user inserts malicious JavaScript code into a request sent via Ajax, which is then executed on the user's browser without their knowledge. To mitigate this risk, it is important to carefully validate all data sent via Ajax and encode it correctly to prevent the execution of malicious code.

Another risk to consider is related to Cross-Site Request Forgery (CSRF) attacks. In a CSRF attack, a malicious user exploits the active session of a legitimate user to send malicious requests to the server, for example to make an unauthorized money transfer. To prevent this type of attack, it is essential to use anti-CSRF tokens in Ajax requests to verify the authenticity of the user before performing a sensitive operation.

It is also important to protect communications between the client and server when using Ajax. To ensure the confidentiality and integrity of exchanged data, it is advisable to use secure HTTPS connections and encrypt sensitive data transmitted via Ajax. This way, the risk of malicious data interception is prevented, and it ensures that the information exchanged between the client and server is protected.

To further increase the security of web applications using Ajax, it is recommended to implement robust authentication and authorization mechanisms. For example, protocols like OAuth can be used to manage access to protected resources and ensure that only authorized users can access the application's sensitive features.

Lastly, it is important to conduct regular security analyses on the source code of the web application to identify any vulnerabilities and fix them promptly. By using static and dynamic code analysis tools, potential security issues related to the use of Ajax can be identified, and appropriate countermeasures can be adopted to mitigate risks.

In conclusion, if used correctly and with proper precautions, Ajax can help improve user experience on the web and make applications more dynamic and interactive. However, it is essential to pay attention to security during the development of web applications using Ajax in order to protect sensitive data and prevent potential cyber attacks.

21. Practical Exercise: Creating a web application that uses Ajax to handle data update requests

Creating a web application that uses Ajax to handle data update requests is a very important process to improve user experience and optimize site performance. In this article, we will provide you with a detailed guide on how to create a web application with Ajax to handle data update requests.

First of all, it is important to understand what Ajax is and how it works. Ajax, acronym for Asynchronous JavaScript and XML, is a technology that allows sending and receiving data from the server without having to reload the entire web page. This means that specific parts of the page can be updated asynchronously, without interrupting the user experience.

To create a web application with Ajax, you

need to know at least three fundamental components: HTML, CSS, and JavaScript. HTML is used to create the structure of the web page, CSS to define the style of the page, and JavaScript to add interactivity and handle Ajax requests.

Here is a basic example of HTML code to create a simple web page that will use Ajax to handle data update requests:

```html
<!DOCTYPE html>
<html>
<head>
    <title>Web Application with Ajax</title>
    <script src="https://ajax.googleapis.com/ajax/libs/jquery/3.5.1/jquery.min.js"></script>
</head>
```

```html
<body>
    <div id="content">
        <!-- Updated data through Ajax will be displayed here -->
    </div>
    <script>
        // defining the function that sends the Ajax request to the server
        function updateData() {
            $.ajax({
                url: 'update_data.php',
                type: 'GET',
                success: function(data) {
                    $('#content').html(data);
                },
                error: function(xhr, status, error) {
                    console.log('An error occurred during the request: ' + error);
```

```
        }
      });
    }


    // update data every few seconds
    setInterval(updateData, 5000); // update every 5 seconds
  </script>
</body>
</html>
```

In the above HTML code, we have created a basic web page with a `<div>` with the ID "content," which will be used to display the updated data from the server through Ajax. We have also included the jQuery library to simplify the use of Ajax.

After opening the `<script>` tag, we have defined a function `updateData()` that sends an Ajax request to the server using the `$.ajax()` method. The server will respond with the updated data, which will be displayed inside the `<div>` with the ID "content."

Finally, we have used the `setInterval()` function to call the `updateData()` function every 5 seconds to keep the data always updated on the page.

Once you have created the basic HTML code, you need to implement the server-side code that will handle the data update requests. In this example, let's assume we are using PHP as the server-side language and creating a file called "update_data.php" that will return the updated data:

```php
<?php
```

```php
// simulating a data update operation
$new_data = 'New updated data: ' . date('Y-m-d H:i:s');
echo $new_data;
?>
```
```

The PHP code simply returns a string containing the current date and time as the updated data. In a real web application, this code should actually update the data from the database or other data sources.

Once you have created both the HTML and PHP code, you can test the web application by opening the HTML file in your browser. You should see the text "New updated data: [current date and time]" displayed inside the `<div>` with the ID "content," and the data will be automatically updated every 5 seconds without having to reload the entire page.
```

Index

1. Introduction to AJAX pg.4

2. Knowledge required to use AJAX pg.7

3. Simple Interactions in AJAX pg.11

4. Advanced interactions in AJAX pg.16

5. Callback, XMLHttpRequest, asynchronous in Ajax pg.33

6. examples of Callback, XMLHttpRequest, asynchronous in Ajax pg.38

7. Event Management in Ajax pg.41

8. Error Handling in Ajax pg.45

9. Cross-browser compatibility in Ajax pg.53

10. Methods in AJAX pg.59

11. Parameters in AJAX pg.66

12. Implementation of Ajax in JavaScript pg.71

13. Using jQuery to simplify the implementation of Ajax pg.79

14. Using front-end frameworks to handle Ajax calls pg.83

15. Parameters in AJAX pg.89

16. Monitorare AJAX con PHP pg.94

17. Monitoring AJAX with ASP.NET Data submission (GET and POST) pg.99

18. Database clienti di Ajax. pg.106

19. AJAX User Side and Server Side pg.114

20. Security and Analysis in Ajax pg.119

21. Practical Exercise: Creating a web application that uses Ajax to handle data update requests pg.122

www.ingramcontent.com/pod-product-compliance
Lightning Source LLC
Chambersburg PA
CBHW050305230526
45471CB00005B/2026